PARADISE PARK AFTER DARK

Written by Farah Downing & Illustrated by Holly Monger

Pink flamingoes fandango
Along the rope-bridge for a thrill
While hummingbirds so*ar*, sw*oop*
And L**oo**p the l**oo**p until -

But

Penguins

prefer a

wave so

The blue slide is their best

They surf d o w n, pl u n g e and paddle

Among the balls in two tone vests

Camouflaged, the Parrots preen

And polish their bony beaks,

Perched to watch the creatures

Reach a kaleidoscope peak.

An ark full of animals fetch

Their mats to make the climb

And there, laid like a tea party
On tables for the take –
There's Sandwiches and cakes,
Crisps, Fizzy-pop, ice-creams
So they crunchy munch the lot

What a truly delicious dream!

Otter full and first to finish.

DI**V**ES in the ball pool for a play

Red panda is the next to go.

He scales a rope and swings away

The goats and sheep clamber
Climb, bleat and SHRIEK
Playing tag, forty – forty,
And even hide 'n' seek.

Playtime becomes party time,
As pigs turn the music HIGH
And oinking to the rhythm their
Feathered friends take to the sky.

But before they know it, Owl hoots out a warning,
Cockerel crows the message on,

TWIT TWOO

COCK A

DOODL

"QUICK IT'S NEARLY MORNING!"

A miniature steam engine,
Chuffs up and waits outside,
With donkey as driver
They climb aboard their ride.

Feathers fluster, hooves tap,
Furry ears a-twitch,
The animals settle <u>down</u>
And donkey **HITS** the switch.

The animals settle for a sleepy day.

For they've been up all night in the barn to play

Goodnight

Sleep tight

The Place
Paradise Park is Cornwall's top wildlife sanctuary and indoor Jungle play barn. It is also home to the world Parrot Trust an international organisation that works to protect and conserve the world's parrot population.

The Author
Farah Downing writes stories for children. She is also a mum and a teacher.
Farah loves being silly, swimming, beach days and muddy walks.
Her favourite things are chocolate and new pencils.
She lives in St Ives with her family.

The Illustrator
Holly Monger draws pictures and colours them in. She loves the seaside, reading books and getting messy with paint and ink.
Her favourite things are breakfast cereal and new colouring pencils.
She lives in London but grew up near the beach in Cornwall.

All rights reserved. No part of this publication may be reproduced, converted or archived into any other medium without relevant permission first being obtained from the publisher. Nor should the book be circulated or resold in any binding other than its original cover.

Paradise Park, After Dark

Text: © Farah Downing
Illustrations: © Holly Monger

First Edition published 2012

Printed & Published by:
The St Ives Printing & Publishing Company,
High Street, St Ives, Cornwall TR26 1RS UK.

www.stivesnews.co.uk

ISBN: 978-0-948385-60-5